Original title:
Cacti in the Moonlight

Copyright © 2025 Creative Arts Management OÜ
All rights reserved.

Author: Miriam Kensington
ISBN HARDBACK: 978-1-80581-891-5
ISBN PAPERBACK: 978-1-80581-418-4
ISBN EBOOK: 978-1-80581-891-5

Nighttime's Gentle Embrace on Arid Souls

Under the silver glow so bright,
Spiky guardians dance in the night.
They wear sombreros, oh so sly,
While neighbors wonder, 'What's their tie?'

With a wink from the moon, they prance,
Each cactus taking a funny stance.
One wobbles, almost falls down,
Declaring, 'Showbiz! I'm the talk of the town!'

Illuminating the Resilient Green

Sunbaked jokes in the cool of night,
Spikes and laughter, a wondrous sight.
They have parties with stars, you see,
"Pass the water!" they bubble with glee.

One jester cactus wears a bow,
"Will this dance impress, or make you go 'whoa?'"
He spins and giggles, peer through the haze,
While the moon chuckles, lost in its gaze.

Mystic Shadows on Desert Prickles

In shadows cast, the fun begins,
Sharp little fellows with giant grins.
They share tickles with the gentle breeze,
"Oh, don't be prickly, laugh with me, please!"

A taco party? Why, don't mind!
Arranged on shelves of tangled vine!
Every bite's a spectacle loud,
And then they pop like popcorn proud!

Stardust Amongst the Desert's Hold

With stardust sprinkled on green attire,
Each spiky friend ignites a choir.
"Who knew night could tickle your heart?"
With every giggle, they play their part.

They sway like dancers, a ridiculous sight,
Challenging the moon for the best spotlight.
"What's the punchline?" one shouts with glee,
While the desert giggles, wild and free.

Moonlit Conversations in Dried Earth

Underneath the silver glow,
Silly shadows dance and flow.
Plant debates in cheeky tones,
Who needs friends when we have thorns?

The lizards laugh, the owls hoot,
As we argue who's more cute.
A prickly joke goes around,
And yet, not a soul is found.

Nightfall Reveries in Sandy Groves

Old spines gossip, tales they tell,
'Remember last year's rain? Oh well!'
Sandstorms come and whisk away,
  Our dry humor saves the day.

The stars wink, they join the fun,
While moonlit pranks have just begun.
An agile fox, a startled quail,
  We giggle softly, never pale.

The Luminous Thorns of Dusk

When dusk arrives, we shine so bright,
Our prickles glitter, what a sight!
Cacti chuckles fill the air,
Beware the ones who dare to stare!

'Your style's sharp!' one plant declares,
'But look at that guy's wild hairs!'
Dancing shadows, we poke fun,
In this desert, we're number one!

A Prayer to the Desert Stars

Oh stars above, so far yet near,
How many jokes do you hear?
As thorns poke laughter in the breeze,
We thrive on humor with such ease.

In the silence, giggles rise,
'Who's the prickliest?' our question flies.
With moonlight's glow, we stand in pride,
Together, friends, we do abide.

Silent Vigil of the Desert Planters

Under the stars they stand so still,
Guarding the night with a quirky thrill.
Each one dressed in prickly attire,
Whispering jokes by the cool campfire.

With shadows tall and laughter wide,
Their spines poking fun, they can't hide.
Dance of the desert with a cheeky cheer,
Planting the seeds of giggles here.

The Moon's Embrace on Spiky Souls

In the moonlight, they wave and sway,
Prickly pals having a laugh-filled play.
With arms outstretched, their needles gleam,
Telling tales of a desert dream.

The silver beams bring out their puns,
As they share stories of silly runs.
Who knew being sharp could be so fun?
Dancing shadows until the sun.

Ethereal Nightfall Over Sandy Sentinels

In the quiet dark, their humor spikes,
Beneath the moon, they tell of bikes!
One cactus slips, and the others roar,
'Hold it, buddy, that's not a chore!'

With giggles echoing through the dunes,
They swap their tales with playful tunes.
Who knew the night held such glee,
In a landscape of prickly jubilee?

Secrets of the Nocturnal Desert

Whispers rise from the sandy floor,
As secrets spill from each spiky door.
'Last week, I pricked a tumbleweed!'
They laugh so hard, they can't proceed.

The owls hoot loud in night's delight,
As the playful souls share in their plight.
In a world so bright with the moon's embrace,
Even spiky souls find their place.

Monochrome Visions in Desert Stillness

In the still of night, prickly pals stand tall,
Casting shadows, like an awkward ball.
Their arms are raised, as if to say,
"Let's dance! Who cares if it's a new ballet?"

The moonlight glints on their spiky hats,
While lizards chuckle, shaking like sprats.
They roll their eyes at the clumsy crew,
For a cactus can't dance; that's just not what they do!

A breeze comes by, teasing them slight,
"Try a cha-cha, but hold on tight!"
The thorns get tangled in a misstep,
Resulting in cacti snoring: "Take a nap, not a step!"

Yet in this desert, where giggles bloom,
Even the stars chuckle at the looming doom.
So let them sway under skies so vast,
For even tough plants can have a laugh at last!

A Dance Beneath the Starlit Canopy

Beneath the stars, a prickly parade,
Swirls of green in a moonlit charade.
With formations flailing, they bob and weave,
"Look at us dance! Or maybe just grieve?"

Saguaro takes the lead, in a comical trance,
With moves so stiff, it's hard not to prance.
While others join in, with wobbly flair,
Two left feet? They just don't care!

A tumbleweed rolls, joining the fun,
"Watch my spin!" it shouts, "A daring run!"
But as it swirls, it gets stuck on a spire,
And everyone gasps—"Oh no, he's on fire!"

But laughter erupts, in the cool, crisp air,
As they try to help with a delicate care.
In the land of the night, where quirks can thrive,
Even in stillness, they keep the joy alive!

Tales Woven by Twilight and Flora

Under a starry grin, the shadows dance,
Prickly pals winking in a leafy trance.
Shedding their troubles with a playful twirl,
Even the thorns join in the midnight whirl.

Whispers of secrets in the cool night air,
As giggles of greens float without a care.
They tell of dreams caught in the lunar beams,
While wiggly roots weave the funniest schemes.

The moon plays tricks on their prickly hats,
Sprinkling confetti on jovial chats.
With every poke of a spiky cheer,
They scatter laughter that all can hear.

So gather 'round, let the night unfold,
With tales of the daring—so goofy and bold.
In the realm of the goofy under moonlight,
The flora's frolic turns the dark to bright.

Night's Mirage Among the Resilient

In shadows so thick, the laughter grows wide,
Resilient wonders with smiles as their guide.
Each spike a jest, each flower a laugh,
Living their lives like a comedy staff.

The nightly parade of odd shapes and hues,
Swirling about, like a dance of the blues.
While the moon stifles a giggle, oh what a sight,
As they strut about, claiming the night.

Puns on their petals, a sight to behold,
Quirky companions, so brave and so bold.
With a chuckle and chortle, they poke at the sky,
Making the world wonder why they fly high.

As the stars twinkle light on the spiky brigade,
Each throws a wink, unafraid and unmade.
In this mirage where laughter is free,
The resilient dreamers find joy in the spree.

Beneath the Veil of Dawn's Approaching

As dawn tiptoes in on a fuzzy bright shoe,
The plants come alive with a giggling crew.
They stretch and they yawn, but oh, what a sight,
With arms wide open to greet the new light.

Jumpy and bouncy with humor intact,
The thorns play tag, it's a silly contract.
Beneath the bright rays, the fun starts to peak,
In the dance of the dawn, they play hide and seek.

With a wiggle and jiggle, they scatter around,
Unfurling the joy that's lost to be found.
The sun cracks a grin, it knows what to do,
While the goofy plants cheer in a flourish of hue.

So here's to the laughter beneath the dawn's gaze,
To spirits awakened in jovial ways.
Each plant wears a smile that's woven with cheer,
Creating a meadow of humor sincere.

Awakening the Spirit in the Moon's Glow

Under the moonlight, the mischief unfolds,
With spirits of greenery, both quirky and bold.
In the shimmering glow, they gather and grin,
As the night casts a spell—a wild, joyful din.

They poke and they prod at the silence of night,
Giggles escape as they frolic in flight.
Each leaf is a story, each flower a jest,
Celebrating the evening—they're truly the best.

The moon looks down with a gleeful surprise,
At the riot of colors that dance in the skies.
Silly shadows bounce and hop to the beat,
In the glow of the twilight, they twirl on their feet.

So let's join the laughter of this leafy delight,
Under the silver that softens the night.
In this magical realm where the spirits all play,
The beauty of joy lights the silliest way.

Guardians of the Desert Under Stars

In desert nights, we stand so tall,
With spiny arms, we have a ball.
The coyotes howl, we dance around,
A prickly party is what we've found.

Watch our shadows, they wiggle and sway,
While we chuckle softly in a quirky way.
The stars above seem to feign surprise,
As we poke each other—no one denies.

A tumbleweed rolls, we laugh so loud,
Who knew sharp fellows could be so proud?
The moonlight glimmers on our thorny skin,
We toast to the night with a joke or win.

Oh how we guard this sandy expanse,
While snakes slither by, we still find a chance.
To share a giggle, to spread some cheer,
Even in dryness, we hold fun dear.

The Soft Light on Sharp Edges

In soft light glows, we seem so nice,
But gents beware, we're not just a slice.
With prickle knights, we fight the plight,
Guarding our turf with all our might.

A lizard slides past, he makes us laugh,
With silly antics, he splits the path.
Oh, prickly friends, put on a show,
With sharp-edged spins and a wobbly flow.

A sand dune rolls, we act like it's game,
Chasing our shadows, we stake our claim.
Under the stars, we share a good jest,
Our edges are sharp, but we're still the best.

We whisper secrets and giggle aloud,
The desert's ours, we feel quite proud.
In the soft light hour, don't take it to heart,
We may be prickly, but here's the art.

Parables of the Desert at Night

Listen up, friends, to tales of the night,
When we stand tall, it's quite the sight.
Hooting owls join with our prose,
As moonbeams tickle our sharp little toes.

A rabbit hops by, what a curious glance,
We make silly faces, invite him to dance.
With wisdom of plants and tales to be told,
Our humor unfolds, never gets old.

A scorpion crawls, showing off its sting,
We laugh at the antics of scaly little things.
We share our quirks, we share our charm,
Even the desert finds joy in our calm.

So gather around for stories quite wild,
Of spines and smiles, we've all been beguiled.
With every chuckle beneath the bright skies,
Let humor blossom; it never denies.

Kaleidoscope of Shadows and Silhouettes

Shadows dance under the lunar glow,
Creating shapes that playfully flow.
We twist and turn, a sharp silhouette,
In a comic play, we have no regret.

The night critters join our wild parade,
With laughter echoing, plans quickly made.
Who knew that prickly could also be fun?
Outside the dark, we shine like the sun.

Silhouettes prance in a wobbly groove,
The desert floor feels our playful move.
A starlit stage for a quirky night show,
The audience of owls enjoy our flow.

Our tales sprinkle joy like desert rains,
Under milky skies, humor never wanes.
So laugh with us under this quilt so vast,
For shadows and smiles make the night last.

Echoes of the Dunes at Dusk

In the twilight, sand dunes sway,
A tumbleweed joins the ballet,
With a hop and a skip, it prances,
Making shadows do funny glances.

Stars giggle in the evening sky,
While lizards in shades wear ties,
A whispering breeze tells a joke,
As moonlit critters join the smoke.

The owls hoot at a punchline's peak,
While foxes gather, all unique,
Their laughter rings through the arid night,
In this desert, everything's just right.

In the distance, a jackrabbit frets,
Worrying over his tux and pets,
But what's style in this sandy ballet?
As the dunes roll on, just let them play.

The Midnight Dance of Spines

Under stars, a party unfolds,
Where prickly dancers break the molds,
Spines shake and twirl, so full of glee,
A forest of laughter—come see, come see!

Beneath the moon, the puns take flight,
With each jig and wiggle, a funny sight,
They bump and grind like they've got no fears,
Swaying like tumbleweeds, oh what cheers!

A tarantula DJ spins the tracks,
While other bugs converge in packs,
The beat drops low, and they all unite,
In this peculiar, joyful night.

When dawn arrives, they hide away,
Leaving laughter and clumsiness to stay,
A secret shared in whispers low,
Of dancing spines, and the moon's glow.

Celestial Reflections on Sandy Skin

Glimmering grains under starlit wit,
Dunes showcase a comedy skit,
The shadows peek, then slide and slip,
As laughter echoes in the light's trip.

A scorpion sidesteps in fancy shoes,
With every leap, it sings the blues,
Sand beneath, stars all around,
Joyful giggles echo from the ground.

Lizards wear hats, oh what a sight,
As they groove on by, feeling quite light,
Each reflection reveals a cheeky grin,
Mirth so contagious, let's all join in!

Sunrise will come, but hold that thought,
For sand-dusted giggles can't be caught,
In the desert's fun, we find our skin,
Where gleeful secrets deep within begin.

Secrets of Desert Flora Under the Moon

Flora whispers secrets to the night,
As petals open, simple delight,
Each bloom a prankster, clever and sly,
Playing tricks as the stars dance by.

Behind a rock, a flower grins,
For in the dark, mischief begins,
A silly sprout tickles the sand,
While others cheer, a grand band.

The moonlight giggles, casting its glow,
Reflecting fun in the flowers row,
With every petal, a tale unfolds,
In this comedy where nature scolds.

But worry not, for dawn's embrace,
Will blanket the night's funny face,
Until then, under this lunar boon,
Let's laugh together, dance 'til noon.

Silvered Spines Beneath Stars

In the desert night, they sway,
With pointy hats, they dance and play.
A prickly party, oh what a sight,
Stealing moonbeams, feeling just right.

Each puffed up friend wears a grin,
Under the glow, they'll never thin.
Twisting and turning with cactus flair,
Spinning tales that float in the air.

Around a fire, they gather near,
Complaining 'bout nights that are too clear.
At just the right angle, shadows tease,
Sprouting laughter on warm desert breeze.

With silver spines in the night's embrace,
They ponder life at a pokey pace.
In a world of sand and a chuckling moon,
It's a prickly jam, oh it's coming soon!

The Midnight Oasis

Beneath the stars, a cocktail bar,
With spiky drinks that'll raise the bar.
Sip the nectar, take a chance,
In this oasis, all plants can dance!

The palms sway low, the drinks are bright,
A rumble erupts, oh what a sight!
A tumbleweed rolls on the floor,
Trying to join, but falling more!

Laughter echoes through the flora,
As they toast to quirks and explorer auras.
With wild ideas and tales so sly,
The frosty night twinkles as they fly.

It's a midnight gathering, they conspire,
Under the stars, hearts catch fire.
No need for rules or fancy attire,
Just prickle and laugh until they tire!

Ghostly Flora

In the moonlight, shadows take flight,
With ghostly blooms, oh what a sight!
These flowery phantoms, they're quite a crew,
Floating about with a cheeky hue.

Whispers bounce off the prickly spines,
Spooking the night with their silly lines.
"Don't be scared, we're just here to play!"
They twinkle under moonbeams, come what may.

With long-lost roots and wild histories,
Telling tales of cactus mysteries.
A jolly lot, beware their tricks,
Their laughter echoes, it really sticks!

So if you wander under night skies,
And hear them giggle, don't be surprised.
They're just some spirits having a ball,
In the garden of dreams where echoes call!

Moonscape Garden

Under the stars in a garden rare,
Where peculiar plants show off their flair.
With a twirl and twist, they wave so spry,
While the moon chuckles from the sky.

Giggling sprouts with a mischievous grin,
Challenge the night with playful spin.
"Come dance with us, oh wanderer bold!"
In a patch of laughter, it never gets old.

The moon beams down with a knowing wink,
As the flora plots and sips a drink.
Beneath the glow, life's a merry game,
Where every night feels a little the same.

In the moonscape garden, all are friends,
With jests and giggles that never ends.
So join the fun in the glow so bright,
Embrace the joy of a starry night!

Dance of the Silent Sentinels

In shadows tall, they sway like pros,
With prickly tips and pointy toes.
They boogie under the starry dome,
Each sway a giggle, far from home.

Their green arms flail in lunar beams,
As if they're lost from vibrant dreams.
But watch them carefully, my friend,
For even plants need time to blend.

Whispers in the Dry Air

Listen close, they gossip low,
About the wind, the sun, the snow.
With spiny laughter—they poke and tease,
Making the night dance with such ease.

Who knew they had a cheeky side?
Beneath the stars, they take great pride.
A silent roar, a fateful jest,
In this dry air, they're all the best!

Evening's Embrace of the Arid

As dusk falls down, they strike a pose,
With arms wide open, their stance it shows.
A little shy, yet full of flair,
They wear the night; it's quite the wear.

They giggle softly in their green skin,
Playing hide and seek with the moon's grin.
In this embrace, they dance with glee,
Who knew dryness could be so free?

Oasis of Resilience

Amidst the sands, they thrive and play,
With spiky crowns, quite the display.
They joke about thorns while sipping dew,
In a vibrant world, they make their due.

An oasis of smiles in a barren land,
With every breeze, they take a stand.
They bloom with laughter, a quirky spree,
In their own way, they're wild and free!

Glistening Refuge Under Silent Skies

Under a blanket of velvet blue,
Prickly friends dance in the dew.
They wiggle and sway, all in delight,
Inviting stars for a silly night.

With laughter that echoes, they share their jokes,
While wise old owls exchange their pokes.
In the glow of the moon, they grow so spry,
Who knew sharp things could be so sly?

Each thorny lad dons a shimmering hat,
Beneath twinkling gems, they engage in chat.
They tell tales of storms, high winds, and cheer,
In a land where not much happens here.

So tiptoe softly, don't make a sound,
These funny green pals are joyfully bound.
Under the stars with such silly flair,
A party beneath, above thrills the air.

Serpentines of Light in the Nightscape

In shadows they shimmy, oh what a sight,
Their spines catching moons, glowing so bright.
With laughter like water, a stream of glee,
They throw a wild bash, just you and me.

Each twist and turn brings another surprise,
As wisecracking critters roll up their eyes.
With jokes fluttering, a breezy affair,
We dance with the spines without any care.

Under the cosmos, they revel and play,
Doing the cha-cha with not much to say.
With every sharp jab, a chuckle does bloom,
While stars overhead form a shimmery room.

Entwined in the magic of nighttime's embrace,
These prickly delights put smiles on our face.
As dawn creeps in, with a wink and a plume,
They giggle goodnight, then head to their room.

Nocturnal Portraits of Sun-kissed Spines

Framed by the night in a quirky array,
Sun-kissed charmers come out to play.
With a brush of the moon, they paint their tale,
Imagine a clown on a ship's crooked sail.

With piquant quips under starlit skies,
These cheeky enthusiasts wear laughter's guise.
Their spines like confetti, poke fun at the dark,
From shadows they leap with a sparkling lark.

They whisper of dreams, both silly and bold,
With spines throwing shade, but never too cold.
As the night rolls on in a shimmering dance,
Their jests bring us joy, if given a chance.

Oh, if you join in their giggles so sweet,
You'll find prickly friends you can't help but greet.
Under full moons that brighten the scene,
These fellows remind us: life's not too keen.

Sibilant Night in the Desert Expanse

A sibilant hush drapes the wide open land,
While spiny companions form quite the band.
With comedic flair, they puff and they poke,
In prickly pajamas, they laugh and they joke.

The cacti sway low, like dancers in charade,
Mimicking giants that drink lemonade.
With shadows that giggle and echo their mirth,
A tuneful connection floats over the earth.

Amidst the stars, they initiate fun,
With jests flitting 'round under bright blazing sun.
Their nocturnal talents keep spirits afloat,
In this sandy expanse, they dance and gloat.

As dawn peeks slowly, with yawns and nice dreams,
These spiky dear pals conspire with beams.
What laughter they share in the cool of the night,
In a world that's not sleepy but brimming with light.

Whispers of Wisdom in Desert Flora

Underneath the twinkling skies,
Spiky folks with wise old eyes.
They ponder life with a steady gaze,
And tell the tales of desert ways.

With needles sharp, they throw a jab,
At any critter trying to grab.
The lizards laugh, the owls hoot,
While cactus sages share their loot.

In their silence, quirks reside,
Sending ripples of giggles wide.
Who knew plants could have such fun,
Plotting pranks under the sun?

When the breeze begins to dance,
Those prickly ones take a chance.
They sway and shimmy, a sight so rare,
Stealing laughs from the desert air.

Night's Palette on Prickled Leaves

When shadows fall and stars ignite,
The prickles share a silly sight.
Dancing in their spiky shoes,
They boast of colors no one views.

A moonbeam hits a barrel's grin,
While saguaro strikes a pose, so thin.
The night unfolds its art display,
With giggles echoing all the way.

The glow of pale lights brings they cheer,
And soon the desert's full of cheer.
With every twist and crazy dance,
These prickly pals defy their stance.

In this wild, nocturnal show,
Petals blushing, putting on a glow.
So here's to laughter, fun, and glee,
Among the thorns, who'd thought it'd be?

Moonlit Guardians of the Arid Sea

Beneath the moon's watchful eye,
Prickly sentinels stand up high.
They guard the dunes with flair and style,
In their own, hilarious, poky smile.

With every gust of wind, they sway,
Making fun of the night's ballet.
The stars above snicker and wink,
At these guardians that play and blink.

A javelina trips on a thorn,
Then the laughter starts to adorn.
In the stillness, a chuckle creeps,
As sleeping critters bait their sleeps.

When the darkness finally fades,
Their antics leave a trail of shades.
For in this land where fun's a must,
The moonlit guardians find their trust.

Enchanted Flora Beneath Cosmic Gaze

In the hush of night, they conspire,
Plucky plants with dreams of fire.
Under cosmic glimmers, they play,
With glitter twinkling on their way.

"Look at me!" a tiny bloom shouts,
As starry friends erupt in doubts.
"I'm the queen of the desert realm!"
While others roll their eyes and overwhelm.

The tumbleweeds join in the song,
Spinning tales about what's wrong.
They dance through shadows, full of cheer,
With every turn, they draw us near.

So under stars, the laughter flows,
Among the pads and spiky rows.
In this enchanted, quirky night,
The flora makes the whole world bright.

Ethereal Flora Dance

In the desert night, they sway so spry,
With arms like dancers reaching high.
Prickly pals in a moonlit trance,
Begging for a moonlit chance.

They wiggle and jiggle, a comical sight,
Under the stars, with all their might.
Pointy shoes tap on the sandy ground,
In this wacky party, joy abounds.

Sipping on starlight, they laugh with glee,
Making fun shadows, oh so carefree.
Spines in a whirl, they can't help but prance,
Who knew our friends could dance this dance?

When the sun peeks in, they freeze in place,
Like awkward kids caught in a race.
But come night again, watch them advance,
These ethereal flora, lost in their dance.

Luminescent Arid Dreams

Under a blanket of shimmering cream,
Silly green thorns, they plot and scheme.
Daytime rainbows turn into stunts,
While dreaming of tacos and wild, funky fonts.

In the sandy terrain, they proudly boast,
Of nighttime parties and cactus toast.
With a wink and a nod, they share tales bold,
Of mischief made when the night sky's gold.

Sipping the moonlight from glistening mugs,
Giggling at shadows, giving out hugs.
Each little spine a comedian's flair,
With tales of the desert thrown in the air.

As dawn starts to break, the antics recede,
They stand tall and silent, no longer freed.
But the night will return, full of sunny schemes,
To see those green pals in luminescent dreams.

Twilight in the Desert

As twilight falls, they stretch with grace,
Little stunt performers in their own space.
Twinkling lights sparkle in potted plants,
Cactus clowns do their night-time dance.

A moonlit serenade plays high and sweet,
While spiky pals shake to the rhythm of feet.
They trade cactus jokes with a comical air,
Tickling the sands, spreading joy everywhere.

With whimsical stories and giggles galore,
Inventing new moves, yearning for more.
Their spines are a shield, but tonight they cheer,
For at least once a week, they conquer their fear.

As the deep dark night wraps around,
The laughter of plants is the only sound.
When day breaks the fun, they simply retreat,
But come twilight again, they'll return to compete.

Serene Thorns

In peaceful gardens where shadows blend,
Chillin' all night with a prickly friend.
Serene vibes flow, an unimaginable thrill,
As starry-eyed greens tackle twilight chill.

With spines so sharp, they play hide and seek,
Behind rocky shadows, so shy and sleek.
Guffaws erupt, as they tumble and roll,
These serene thorns reveal their true soul.

Sipping on sunshine, they poke fun at fate,
Wearing floral hats that are way out of date.
Jokes about water, a universal theme,
In the land of the spiny, it's all but a dream.

When dawn calls them back to their chair,
They wave goodnight, without a care.
But at night's return, with splashes of tone,
These serene thorns make laughter their own.

Night Blooming Wonders

In shadows deep, they spread their arms,
With humorous charms, they cause alarms.
Dancing in the glow of silver beams,
They wink at stars, fulfilling dreams.

Each bloom a face, quirky and bright,
Giggles erupt in the still of night.
Their thorns like jokes, sharp but so sweet,
Turning the desert into a treat.

Underneath the wide and twinkling sky,
They throw a party as night rolls by.
Balloons of pollen, laughter in air,
A gathering of mischief, beyond compare.

So here's to blooms that come out to play,
Wonders of night, hip-hip-hooray!
With every petal, a punchline shared,
In the moon's spotlight, hilarity bared.

Starlit Prickles

Prickly friends under cosmic lights,
They crack jokes that tickle the nights.
A dance-off with shadows, what a sight,
Bouncing to rhythms of joyous delight.

With their funny hats and pointy shoes,
They throw a bash, no time to snooze.
Poking fun at the passing breeze,
Who knew being sharp could be such a tease?

In every corner, laughter spouts,
As starry gossip fills the night shouts.
Jokes are a-flutter like firefly dreams,
Funny little pricks, or so it seems.

So come join the fest, don't be a fool,
Under the stars, we break all the rules.
With giggles of thorns and winks full of cheer,
These prickly pals ignite the atmosphere.

Solitary Sentries

Guardians of fun in the quiet of night,
Standing so still, yet full of delight.
With arms crossed, they hold their ground,
But oh, the giggles, they spread around.

Each holds a secret, a pun on the side,
They snicker and chuckle, but try to hide.
Their stoic stance tells quite the tale,
Of wild escapades that never grow stale.

In the stillness, they whisper and grin,
Sharing old tales over a soft wind's spin.
They tell of the day when they played tag with light,
And how they once danced under a meteor's flight.

So let them guard with their quirky ways,
Beneath the wide skies, laughter stays.
Their watchful eyes spark joy in the dark,
Solitary sentries, igniting the spark.

Dreaming Under Palms

In the midst of palms, the jokes take flight,
As quiet shadows greet a vibrant night.
Giggles erupt from the sandy floor,
In this funny land, who could ask for more?

Bouncing dreams drift on sleepy winds,
With every rustle, the funny begins.
"What's green and prickly?" one cheeky palm,
Answers arise with laughter so calm.

Underneath the twinkling starry show,
Dreaming of hijinks where chuckles flow.
With every whisper, a pun crafted tight,
Creating a tapestry of pure delight.

So join the dance in the moonlit breeze,
Where humor grows like a wildflower tease.
Under the palms, a cast of the best,
In a world filled with fun, let's forget the rest.

Prickles and Shadows

In the garden, shadows gleam,
A prickly dance, a funny dream.
The moonlight laughs at hunched-up spines,
While critters tumble o'er the lines.

A chubby critter takes a chance,
In the midst of this spiky dance.
It trips and flips, then makes a scene,
The thorns agree: it's quite the queen!

Shadows stretch like silly yawn,
As if the night is turning dawn.
Prickles poke, yet we don't mind,
With laughter together, we're entwined.

And as they bounce around with glee,
The prickly ones join in the spree.
In the moonlit night, they all unite,
Who knew disguises could be so tight?

Luminous Deserts

Beneath the stars, a desert glows,
With critters dancing on their toes.
A sassy lizard in a tutu prances,
While moonbeams join in all their chances.

A prickly pear starts to complain,
No one respects its spiky reign!
The javelinas come with rubber bands,
To launch their snacks across the sands.

In the bright night, laughter soars,
As the desert springs up open doors.
The luminous sands sizzle and pop,
With quirks enough to make you stop.

Yet through the giggles and silly cheer,
The desert whispers, never fear.
We're all a bit prickly, that is true,
But with moonlight laughs, we're merry too!

Night Whispers Among Succulents

Underneath the starlit sky,
Succulent whispers float and fly.
They giggle softly, trade their jokes,
While dodging the hoots from wandering folks.

A chubby tortoise with a hat,
Joins in their tales and ponders that.
"What's the secret to glowing bright?"
The plants reply, "Just share delight!"

A roguish rat with a painted nose,
Complains that thorns are such a pose.
The agave sighs, "Oh dear, I fear,
But prickles make us truly dear!"

So together they sing, a whimsical tune,
In the soft embrace of the glowing moon.
United they bloom, all feeling bold,
In the night whispers, their stories unfold!

Radiance on Thorny Silhouettes

Silhouettes dance in radiant light,
A prickly party, what a sight!
Thorns are a fashion, they strut with glee,
While shadows morph into quite the spree.

A cholla with flair claims the stage,
As a saguaro starts to engage.
Just watch out for those pointy peeks,
They've got their charm, but oh, those tweaks!

The rattlesnakes do a lively twist,
In the glow they cannot resist.
They jive and shake, causing quite a fuss,
Making sure that none can cuss.

Radiant fun, oh what a thrill,
In this thorny place, there's joy to spill.
So join the dance, let good vibes flow,
In the night's embrace, together we glow!

Pastels of the Dusk on Green Giants

In the twilight glow, they sway and dance,
With floppy hats, they take a chance.
Dressed in shades of pink and green,
They strut around, oh what a scene!

Under the stars, they giggle and sway,
Making up jokes in their own special way.
"Why did the prickly one cross the street?"
"To poke the cactus, now that's a treat!"

As the pastel sky begins to fade,
Those green giants aren't easily swayed.
With laughter spilling in every direction,
They form a party without objection.

In the night air, they spin and twirl,
Wobbling jokes like a dance, oh swirl!
Under the moon, what a joyful sight,
These spiky friends party through the night!

Serenade of Shadows in Thorny Gardens

In the dim-lit patch, they plot and scheme,
Creating shadows, like a silly dream.
With tiny hats and a feather or two,
They serenade the stars, just they and you.

"Oh my, dear friend, do you feel that breeze?"
"Or is it just me, making the leaves tease?"
They break into laughter, a prickly delight,
Sharing rhymes 'til the morning light!

In their thorny abode, a funky mix,
They sing to the sun, with the quirkiest tricks.
Shadows they cast, a whimsical sight,
Rib-tickling tales come alive at night!

Each whispering wind, a playful jest,
In their thorny garden, they joke like the best.
What's a prickly plant's favorite song?
"When I'm in the mood, I sing all night long!"

Celestial Canopy over Desert Dreams

Under the twinkling, starlit skies,
Green creatures gather, oh what a surprise!
Sipping starlight from their favorite cups,
With each sip, oh, how the laughter erupts!

A cactus in shades of midnight blue,
Says, "I could sleep here, how 'bout you?"
The others chime in with a chorus so loud,
"Join the fun, let's dance with the cloud!"

Beneath a moonbeam, they tell tales grand,
Of adventures taken through desert land.
"Did you hear the one about the sneaky sage?
He tried to hug a prickly one on stage!"

As the night deepens, their giggles ignite,
Under cosmic paint, oh what a delight.
Between chuckles and dreams, they sway and beam,
In the celestial glow, life feels like a dream!

Luminescence of Life in the Canyons

In the canyon's embrace, where shadows play,
Prickly pals gather, ready to sway.
With glow-in-the-dark hats and wild shoes,
They start the party, with nothing to lose.

Chortles echo through the rocky space,
The sun dips low, it's the moon's big race.
"Hey, who knew we could light up the night?
Let's dance in the canyons till morning light!"

With luminescent caps, they whirl and spin,
As the stars fall down, let the fun begin!
"Do you think we glow in the day?" one asks,
"With the sun here, we'd be up to our tasks!"

Drifting in laughter, harmonies sway,
Through canyons of life, the merriment stays.
A prickly soirée, wild without fuss,
In the glow of the night, there's no need to rush!

Foraging in the Stardust

Under the stars, we wander wide,
Gathering treasures from nature's side.
A poke here, a tickle there,
Giggles echo in the cool night air.

Jumpy critters with tiny feet,
Join our quest for a midnight treat.
Whispers of snacks and tiny pies,
As space dust twinkles in our eyes.

Silly shadows dance a jig,
As we cartwheel past a friendly twig.
Who knew the night could be so bright?
With laughter ricocheting in moonlight.

So grab your satchel, don't delay,
There's fun to be had in the Milky Way.
We'll forage and smile till morning's call,
In a wacky world, that's a thrill for all.

Phosphorescent Guardians of the Night

Glowing sentinels stand so proud,
Dressed in green, drawing a crowd.
With arms held wide, they wave and sway,
Welcome us in a goofy way.

Their prickles shine like little stars,
Bouncer plants, guarding Mars.
'No trespassing,' they seem to shout,
Yet laughter's how we dance about.

Footloose with friends, we prance and slide,
Around these greens, our goofy guide.
Under the moon's playful glow,
We make silly shadows dance below.

And though the night may seem so still,
We find our fun and share a thrill.
Those guardians smile, yes, they're keen,
To join our fun in this fantastic scene.

Ethereal Prickles in the Moon's Glance

When shadows stretch and giggles blend,
We find the oddest, prickliest friend.
With charm and flair, they stand so tall,
Offering laughs for one and all.

Their spines, a riddle, a funny poke,
Making us chuckle, oh what a joke!
A ticklish brush as we pass by,
Sparkles of humor under the sky.

Swirling breezes play a tune,
Tickling leaves like a witty cartoon.
As night unfolds with a wacky tease,
We roll on laughter, floating like leaves.

From bizarre blooms to odd-shaped trees,
The night's a canvas for quirks like these.
So join the fun, let's dance in jest,
For the joy of life is surely the best!

Whispers of the Desert Under Night's Veil

In the desert's hug, silliness flows,
With whispers of secrets that nobody knows.
Moonlit paths where shadows prank,
In the stillness, we giggle and prank.

Dancing lizards with swaying tails,
Tell us tales of midnight trails.
Chuckling rocks wobble with glee,
As we leap over prickly debris.

The stars above shoot little beams,
Guiding our laughter, igniting dreams.
Each tap of a toe, a tiny spree,
Under the veil of night's decree.

So gather 'round, embrace the night,
With friends who share our silly delight.
For in this land of whimsy and cheer,
The night is ours, let's give a cheer!

Starlit Soliloquy of Desert Flora

Under a sky so bright and bold,
The plants tell tales of nights retold.
With prickly smiles and arms so wide,
They chuckle under the celestial tide.

The shadows dance, a waltz of glee,
As moonbeams tap on cacti with glee.
'Hey there, buddy, don't take it hard,
We're just too cool, we're the desert guard!'

Their spikes are sharp but hearts are light,
Sipping starlight, feeling just right.
They' joke about the passing breeze,
"Is that a tickle or a cactus tease?"

With laughter echoing through the sands,
They share their secrets, exchanging hands.
A funny bunch in the pale moon's glow,
Shimmering stories only they know.

Enigma of the Nocturnal Bloom

In the dark, a riddle takes its stand,
As blooms reveal their secrets, unplanned.
'Why do we bloom when the sun's asleep?'
They giggle softly, their laughter deep.

With petals tucked, hiding from dawn,
The world is their stage, and they are drawn.
"To bloom or not? It's quite a game,
We're nocturnal stars without the fame!"

A flash of color, a side-splitting sight,
"I bet we scare the bats with delight!"
The weeds roll their eyes, sowing their spice,
In an eerie laugh, they think it's quite nice.

So if you wander under the stars,
And hear the blossoms chuckle from afar,
Know it's just the night plants, sly and spry,
Playing tag with dreams that flit by.

The Dance of Shadows Among the Spines

There's a shimmy and shake in the midnight air,
The spiny dancers showing their flair.
With a twist and a turn, a comical sight,
They prance under stars, laughing in the night.

"Watch us wiggle, we're quite the team!
We're the best spiky dancers, or so it would seem!"
They twirl with glee, no fear of a fall,
As shadows get tangled, they're having a ball!

A tumble here, a stab there too,
"Oh dear! That's a prickly rendezvous!"
They giggle as petals take flight in delight,
"Who needs a partner when you've got moonlight?"

So next time you're out and hear their cheer,
Just know they're the stars, so perfectly clear.
"Dance with our shadows, come join the fun,
Underneath the moon, we're the only ones!"

Interviews with the Spiky Spirits

Under the moon, a quirky crew,
Spiky spirits, just waiting for you.
"Tell us your story, we promise to care,
We've gotten some laughs, tangled in hair!"

With pointy jokes, they poke and prod,
"Life's too short, we jest, and nod!"
An interviewer asks, "How's life in the sand?"
"With a side of mischief, it's just grand!"

"What's your secret? How do you thrive?"
"To keep our angles while feeling alive!
Embrace all the quirks, and poke fun at fate,
We're the spiky experts, just don't be late!"

So if you've got questions for those with a grin,
Seek out the spiky, let the laughter begin.
"Life is a jest, under stars so bright,
We'll keep blooming giggles all through the night!"

Slumbering Shadows and Silver Nakedness

In the night, they start to dance,
Tall and prickly, with quite a stance.
Whispers of laughter in the breeze,
Night gnomes giggle behind the trees.

Moonlight glimmers on their skin,
Pointy hats, they sway and spin.
With each twirl, they poke and prance,
Under stars, they take their chance.

A bouncy hop on a grassy hill,
They trip and tumble, oh what a thrill!
With mischievous twinkles in their eyes,
They chase moonbeams, oh how they rise!

As slumber calls and dreams take flight,
Their antics fade into the night.
But when the dawn brings light anew,
They giggle softly, just a few!

Gardens of Thorns Under Cosmic Canopy

In a garden where spines will poke,
Beneath the stars, a funny joke.
Brave little bugs with tiny hats,
Holding parties, oh, imagine that!

Under a sky that sparkles bright,
They toast to thorns with sheer delight.
With blinking lights and jubilant cheer,
The midnight fest, the bugs all near.

A tumbleweed rolls on by,
The sneaky snacks that make them sigh.
They munch on moonlight, laughter blooms,
Amidst the prickles in veiled rooms.

Around they twirl, in sheer excess,
While dodging thorns, it's quite the mess!
As dawn breaks in, they bid their day,
With giggles trailing, frolicking sway.

Encounters in the Moon's Detailed Gaze

In shadows deep, two friends collide,
With spiky hats, no place to hide.
They spin and tumble, what a sight,
Dancing crazily under moonlight.

Oh, what a chance! A fateful bump,
They laugh and bounce, no time to slump.
With pointed friends, they share a grin,
Daring each other to take a spin.

A moonlit race, they dash and dart,
Who knew prickles could win such art?
The laughing stars watch from above,
At this silly chase, filled with love.

As shadows stretch and night winds wane,
They settle down, a bit of strain.
With whistling winds, they'll softly doze,
Until dawn wakes with a warm rosy glow.

Letters to the Stars of the Sandy Realm

In the desert's hush, a note they send,
To twinkling lights, their silly friend.
With points and curves, they scribble fast,
About the shenanigans in sunset's blast.

They laugh at how they dance and sway,
With every bump, they shout hooray!
Each star replies with twinkling cheer,
"You wacky spikers, we hold you dear!"

Bouncing under a cosmic show,
Trying to dodge the tumbleweed flow.
Oh, what adventures await the night,
With cracking smiles, they hold on tight!

As dreams arrive with the morning light,
They vow to send more jokes in flight.
With letters penned in smiles and glee,
The sandy realm sings joyfully!

Alchemy of Light and Thorn

In the night, spines glisten bright,
Dance like fairies in charm and fright.
A green parade with a curious strut,
They tickle the moon, oh what a rut!

Laughter erupts, a prickly jest,
Whispers between the cacti, they jest.
"Why did the aloe cross the blade?"
"To prove his green thumb never swayed!"

With shadows that shimmy on hot desert sand,
Each night, they plot, oh isn't it grand?
Hiccups of laughter, they find quite absurd,
As the night owl hoots, quite undeterred!

Magic blooms in the cool evening air,
With each little poke, they banter and dare.
Hiding their secrets in every thin spine,
Who knew that such plants could be so divine?

Serenity Amidst the Dunes

Under starlit skies, they cozy and chill,
With prickly pals, they enjoy the thrill.
"Hey look at me! I'm a pointy sage!"
"No, you're a cactus stuck in a cage!"

They gossip about the dunes so vast,
Sharing the tales of the travelers past.
"He forgot his map, poor soul went astray,"
"But we've got shade, come what may!"

Breath of night breezes, laughter so clear,
In the desert, there's nothing to fear.
They chuckle and poke with mischievous air,
"Join us dear moon, if you dare to care!"

As shadows play games on the soft sandy bed,
With every soft laugh, their worries are shed.
In this moonlit laughter, hilarity blooms,
A world full of giggles amidst the tombs.

Desert Whispers at Twilight

As daylight fades, tales take flight,
Green heroes gather in twinkling night.
"Whose spine is sharpest? A contest now!"
They boast with gusto, oh, take a bow!

The wise old sage, with spines galore,
Exclaims, "With humor, we flourish more!"
"You think you're tough? Let's have a try!"
They slice through the air with laughter so spry!

Beneath the moon's gaze, they prance and glide,
In this prickly fiesta, no place to hide.
With giggles and pokes, they spin their tales,
Of desert escapades that never fail!

Each whisper of wind, each shake of the ground,
Is filled with a punchline that knows no bound.
In this realm of spikes and playful grace,
Night's merry jesters illuminate space.

Shadows of the Starlit Succulent

In the hush of dusk, shadows extend,
Jokingly poking, with laughter they blend.
"Why do we thrive in this sand so dry?"
"Because we're the plants that know how to fly!"

A triangle of twigs giggle and weave,
Creating tall tales that few can believe.
"I'm a saguaro, so long and tall!"
"But I'm the star, you're just a small wall!"

Flickering lights dance in the invisible breeze,
As the zany potters craft spiky teas.
"Let's host a party, bring out the moon!"
"With its silver glow, we'll dance to a tune!"

So under the stars, with spines all a-quiver,
They swap silly stories, oh what a river!
Laughter echoing through the soft desert air,
In a world made of prickles, who could despair?

www.ingramcontent.com/pod-product-compliance
Lightning Source LLC
Chambersburg PA
CBHW070334120526
44590CB00017B/2878